AF609780

Eden Redefined

Poems

Christine Bode

Praise for Christine Bode and *Eden Redefined*

"From the ravages of limerence to teaching an alien about the taste of pumpernickel, this little book bears the weight of the world. The poems breathe compassion, for self and others, and rage against what disconnects us. Christine writes, "No one was ever there..." But she set her heart and soul on these pages, and I am here for it."

~ *Cathrin Hagey*, Writer and Editor

"*Eden Redefined* teases every sense. Honest and real, the reader will see, hear, feel, taste, and smell the pleasures and pains in Bode's poetic truth. Relatable, raw and refreshing."

~ *Angela Stever*, Author

"*Eden Redefined* is tough to read at times. Christine bares her soul throughout, but this is her trademark: she's an existential mud wrestler, her courage on display, always, even as she despairs. This is admirable...and yet, hope finds its way into her writing, too. Hope and the belief that she belongs in this world. Here. Now. Not because she is an optimist but because she knows she is worthy, knows she is deserving, even as she busies herself scraping despair off her prose-turned-poetry, proving to herself and to us that love and fear can live side-by-side."

~ *Gary William Rasberry*,
Imagination Consultant and Acoustic Entrepreneur

"*Eden Redefined* by Christine Bode is moving, shifting, and potent. Her words touch your emotions right from the start. Bode has the talent to describe a powerful story with just a few words, grabbing your full attention. You will find yourself not stopping until you read the whole book. I loved it very much."

~ *Jacqueline Pirtle*,
Bestselling Author of 365 Days of Happiness, USA

"The light and awareness in these words encourage a potentiality and a will to go on despite the heartbreaks of downward spirals and lost relationships. Christine Bode possesses the ability to touch, show, concern, and console. These poems reveal her insight into experiencing life for what it is, feeling the pain, and having a plan for recovery. With precision, she handles poetic language from the informal to the more esoteric. *Eden Redefined* is well-crafted and a necessary read which allows for our common need to feel."

~ *Kofi Fosu Forson*, Writer and Artist

"Christine Bode has a gift of taking a word, conjuring it into a thread, spinning the words into yarn, and weaving the sentences into tapestries of love, longing, and human truths. Refreshing, honest work."

~ *Marcia Cannon*, Author

"By bravely baring her soul, Christine has taken us on a living journey full of angst, tragedy, love, lust, and longing. We shamelessly eavesdrop on the lamentations of lessons learned then not learned, opportunities found then lost, and loves and lives cut short. In an all too familiar story, we are reminded that we all suffer in the quest for love, acceptance, and validation. We watch her navigate through pandemic isolation in waves of fear, anger, loss, disappointment, and grief. Christine shares her broken yet unsinkable self with us while courageously holding a mirror up to the pain. The often stark and unvarnished language, complete with jaw-clenching honesty, allows us to bear witness to many of life's brutal, precious, heartbreaking and beautifully messy moments, which at times must simply be survived."

~ *Marijane Letourneau*,
Canadian Singer-Songwriter

"Full of passion, vitality, boldness, and inspiration *Eden Redefined* is as startling and audacious in its themes and concepts as it is beautiful and emotive in its language. Brilliant and brave poet Christine Bode knows how to capture the heart like a butterfly in the palm. This vibrant, courageous, and gripping collection of poetry will remind the reader of the frailty of love, life, and happiness and why that fragility is worth experiencing for all its nebulousness."

~ *P.L. Stuart*, Author

Eden Redefined

Poems

Christine Bode

Copyright © 2022 by Christine Bode

All rights reserved.
No portion of this book may be reproduced, stored in a retrieval system, or transmitted in any form or by any means - electronic, mechanical, photocopy, recording, scanning, or other - except for brief quotations in critical reviews, articles, or groups, without written permission of the author/publisher, Christine Bode at bodaciouscopy@gmail.com.

Eden Redefined
Bode, Christine 1964-

ISBN 978-1-7387296-2-3 (Paperback)
ISBN 978-1-7387296-3-0 (eBook)

Edited by Bodacious Copy.
Cover design by Publish and Promote.
Title page photo of Wormsloe, Savannah, Georgia,
by Christine Bode © *2019*

Printed and bound in Canada.

Note to the reader: the information is provided for entertainment purposes only.

To my nieces, Erika Mari-Helena Gagnon and Sarah Lindsay Preston;

My dear friend and lifesaver, Tracie Marko-Hanna, and my brother from another mother, Philip Polk Palmer;

And to:
Tom DiCillo for his graciousness and inspiration.

About the Poet

Christine Anne Bode was born January 14, 1964, in Kingston, Ontario, and is of Celtic/German heritage. She has lived in Toronto and Vancouver and has been writing poetry and song lyrics since she was a teenager. An empath and truth seeker, Christine offers an uninhibited look at her world through her writing and always speaks her truth. She lives in Kingston with her dog.

Christine's first poem, about Shaun Cassidy, was published by Scholastic Book Services in *Rock's Biggest Ten* and in *16 Magazine* in 1978. She was encouraged by a letter from Bob Geldof in 1987 and mentored in the 2000s by Canada's legendary broadcaster, former Chair of the CBC, author, actor and Renaissance man, Patrick Watson.

She is the author of *Eden Refugee*, a collection of visceral street poetry reflecting the experiences of a young woman consumed by sex, drugs, rock'n'roll, unrequited love and a constant quest for spiritual enlightenment, written between 1979 and 2008.

Eden Redefined is Christine's second collection of poetry, written between 2008-2022.

Table of Contents

Reflection

You stared
at me
for a long while from your bar stool in
The Pale.
Silky raven hair
caressing your shoulders,
you kept sweeping it from your
eyes,
dark and wild as a
Connemara pony.
I thought you were the most
beautiful creature
who had ever caught
my gaze,
and marvelled at how I could have
possibly deserved it.

You heard me sing
after several pints and
shots of tequila,
the theme song from
The Mary Tyler Moore Show.
I turned your world on with my smile,
seasoned and stoked
with memories of
Bob Geldof
at Vicar Street

earlier
that evening.

You sat next to me,
spoke in your
soft whispered
hush,
and the next thing I knew
I was in your living room
watching the ever brilliant
Pearl Jam on the TV.
You played
"Yellow Ledbetter,"
and my soul
has never been the same.

More than four years have passed
and I still recall your
passionate words,
furtive glances,
gentle touch,
Scorpion tattoo,
fine patch of soft black chest hair,
the way you loved me
for that moment, and with your heart
held up a mirror
to reflect my beauty,
that which I have only ever understood
through your eyes.
Me, your Hartley. You,
my own Black Irish
Johnny Depp.

A Blessed Morning

This morning I had the good fortune
to wake to the nudging of
my beautiful Goldendoodle's nose,
to stretch, hug her, let her outside to pee,
fill the coffeemaker with water and java,
and turn it on while the sun shines through the window.

A luxurious morning in which to
go back to bed with my coffee—
in a traveller's stainless-steel cup with a lid.
Propping the pillows against the headboard,
I slid under the chocolate-coloured sheets
to read the last fifty-one pages of *Ireland* by
Frank Delaney.

The room rested silent around me
except for
the twittering of spring birds,
the sound of the furnace, and
Scully's breathing as she lay dreaming—
her blonde, curly-furred paws twitching beside me.

The penultimate paragraph of
Delaney's book reads,
"The one joy that has kept me going through life
has been the fact that stories unite us.

And the way we see our story...that's what we own,
no matter who we are and where we come from."

The final paragraph revealed,
"That's why I spent my life as I did –
because that was all I have ever owned,
stories. Indeed, our story is finally
all any of us owns because,
as I once told my grandson,
a story has only one master."

I breathed deeply, closed the book,
rolled over and hugged Scully tight,
inhaling her for a few moments
while staring at the green walls of my bedroom,
and giving thanks to my Master
for a truly blessed morning.

No Idea

You had no idea when you were twenty years old
that the world wouldn't be your oyster;
that you wouldn't become a successful
music video producer and
marry a rock star.

You had no idea when you were twenty-five years old
that the job you landed so easily
with those architects and engineers,
would be the best one
you would ever have.

You had no idea when you were thirty years old
that when you left that excellent job
for an adventure in Vancouver,
the grass wouldn't be greener
although the ocean was.

You had no idea when you were thirty-five years old
that the love you walked away from
two painful years before
would never come again, and
you would always be alone.

You had no idea when you were forty years old
that at the apex of your career
with an entertainment lawyer,

you'd shatter into a million pieces
after your closest cousin's death.

You had no idea when you were forty-five years old
that joyful well-paying jobs and true love
would be so hard to find
in a world where so many middle-aged
single women finish last.

You've no idea what'll happen when you're fifty years old.
You may have become a successful entrepreneur,
you may have met the man of your dreams, and
you may be happier than you could ever have imagined.
You have no idea.

A Season of Sundays

The winter of 2014 shall forever be
remembered
as a season of Sundays,
a day to be both dreaded
and cherished—
family day,
the day I could do
one small thing
to try to help in an impossibly
heartbreaking situation.

During the season of Sundays
I made dinner for my family,
for those of us who could eat—
because my sister
couldn't.
One day, to give my mother
a break
from making meals for
her family
while Karen fought for her life
in a hospital room,
and vomited repeatedly
every single day.

When she could finally come home
and there was nothing else
the doctors could do,
she was a shadow of her
former self—
haunted, terrified, withdrawn—
unable to do anything but
sit on the couch and
listen to us.
All we wanted to do was
be in her presence
for one more day.

These Sundays will never be
enough,
and will never replace
our summers on the river or
shopping with my sisters,
our heart-to-heart conversations or
many family get-togethers, and
every everyday moment and special occasion
we shared
in which she was here and
we were so blessed to have her
with us—
revelling in her beauty and bravery,
cheering her accomplishments,
sharing in her dreams,
knowing full well that she always
deserved centre stage,
and wanting everything she wanted
to be real.

The winter of 2014 shall forever be
remembered
as the season it wouldn't stop
snowing,
the season we tried to hold our emotions at bay,
so we could cope with the
day-to-day cold, wind and icy
fear that gripped our hearts
as we prayed for spring, sunshine, warmth,
new life,
her life—
it's all we ever wanted.

It Is What It Is

I had an epiphany on a rainy, cold spring day,
and was conscious enough to recognize it.
I know what my major life lesson is,
I know now what I am here for.

To understand the meaning of surrender and
to accept that life is loss, pain, and disappointment.
It's how we choose to deal with it and what we take
away from it that matters most.

My sister—my best friend—is dying from ovarian cancer
and there's not a fucking thing I can do about it,
whether I talk about my feelings or don't,
whether you love me and want to help or won't.

You can't bring me solace or hope or faith.
I must walk through this grief alone—as we do—
every time we lose someone we love because
it is what it is, and we can't change it.

Some of us endure tragedy more than others, but
perhaps that's because we are exquisitely blessed with
more people and creatures in our lives that we love,
and for that, we must simply be grateful.

In the past, I chose to self-medicate because
I thought I could not bear the pain.
I thought the food, pot or alcohol would help me cope
with the powerful emotions I was sure would cripple me.

Maybe they did, but this time, I chose to be fully present,
to walk through the ultimate grief and just be with it—
because I know that no matter what anyone says or does,
I can't get out of it—because it is what it is.

Death takes good people who don't deserve to go.
It takes them too soon and too tragically,
leaving behind children, partners, siblings, and friends,
forcing them to figure out how to endure in the face of
profound loss.

I will either accept this with as much presence as I can,
or rant and rave and take my anger out on me, but I don't
deserve that.
I've been through too much already, and I'm too exhausted
to continue to battle against what is not fair.

It is what it is.

The Closest Soul to God

It's the last month of my sister's life,
and I know it.
Tonight, I cried so hard I couldn't see, and
I couldn't breathe.
I cried until the tears streamed down my face and
I choked on my snot.
I cried until the grief in my chest threatened to
inflate me to the most enormous mass of human pain in the
history of the Universe while I begged and pleaded
with God
to send someone to just hold me—
but no one came.
No one was ever there in the early part of the morning,
and no one was there late at night.
No man ever put his arms around me, even once,
in the last six months and told me he'd be there for me
if I needed him because my sister is dying.
Not one single man among all the men I've ever known in
my entire life.

The only being who was there for me every single day of
these twenty-five months of torture is my dog, and she
has borne the weight of my grief, loneliness, and woe,
without complaint or fail or falter.

She lies beside me every night and lets me touch her
and listen to her breathing until I can fall asleep,
giving me the strength I need to face the next day.
She proves that the purpose of every dog in the world is
to teach human beings about the value, strength, and power
of unconditional love.
So, the next time you're about to say to me
(or anyone else) that she's just a dog,
think again,
because she is not just a dog.
She is the closest soul to God I'll ever know.

A Quarter of My Life

I've spent a quarter of my life
wanting to die,
trying not to cry,
crying buckets full of tears,
wrestling with fear.

I've spent a quarter of my life
in a room by myself,
beguiled by music's spell,
walking miles with my dog,
half-blinded by a fog.

I've spent a quarter of my life
lost in the pages of a book,
avoiding the need to cook,
held captive by my dreams,
curbing earsplitting screams.

I've spent a quarter of my life
yearning for true love,
trying to fit inside a glove,
grieving what I've lost,
numbed by sorrow's frost.

I've spent a quarter of my life
cocooned in a movie trance,
not learning how to dance,
talking on the phone,
searching for a home.

I've spent a quarter of my life
loving you with all my heart,
not knowing where to start,
devoid of hope or faith,
so grateful to feel safe.

Menopause Miasma

Almost two months ago, I had a D&C;
my doctor had to burn all the waste out of me.

I'd bled for a year and became so anemic;
I'm telling you, perimenopause is not for the squeamish.

I was so fucking tired, but I had to be strong,
to keep the roof over my head and promote all those songs.

Complex Endometrial Hyperplasia with Atypia
explained that horrendous, never-ending hemorrhage.

I received a total abdominal hysterectomy;
the doc removed all conceptive organs from me.

I didn't mind; I've never needed them anyway, so
now I won't need pap tests, nor will I ever menstruate.

You must look for the silver lining in the clouds
to put up with the gas and constipation of your bowels.

My belly looks like Dr. Frankenstein had at me,
but the staples and stitches have at last been cut free.

Now I'm in menopause, and hot flashes have hit me,
my sleep's more interrupted, and I demand HRT.

I don't have a drug plan which quite sucks the big one,
but I'll give up other luxuries for essential estrogen.

No man could have dealt with what I've gone through,
so if I hear one of you complain about the flu,

I will scream like a banshee at the top of my lungs,
Shut up, you big baby, before I rip out your tongue!

Who Would I Be?

We are what's happened to us.

Who would I be if
I hadn't been overweight since I was eight
If I'd had more self-confidence
If I didn't believe what I was told
If I'd enjoyed exercise more

Who would I be if
I went to university
If I hadn't quit that job in television
If I'd studied photography
If I'd left this place for good

Who would I be if
I had no penchant for bad boys
If I'd said no more than yes
If I didn't like to party
If I'd saved my money from the start

Who would I be if
If my sister hadn't died
If my family hadn't imploded
If I'd laughed more than I cried
If the world wasn't so fucked up

I'd be someone different
But I've no way of knowing
If I'd be better or worse
We all ask, what if
But life isn't for wishing
And there's no hot tub time machine.

We are what's happened to us.

I am who I am
I'm not going to apologize
And I won't live in a land of regret
But I will move forward and carefully choose
Who I will be tomorrow

Parasite

Grief is a parasite,
transmitted by tragedy;
it propels itself down your throat,
shreds a path through your heart
and takes up residence
in your guts.

Parasitism is a relationship
between species in which
the pestilence lives in the host,
causing it to harm as it structurally adapts
to its new environment.

Grief is a parasite
switched to stealth mode,
it rears its ugly head
from the moment you wake,
making you utterly nauseous
for hours every day.

Parasites are predators,
eating their prey slowly,
microscopically so as not to
arouse suspicion—agents of
malaria, dysentery and heartbreak.

Grief is a parasite
growing fat on your pain,
exploiting your trauma,
holding your mind hostage and
modifying your behaviour
for its survival.

Parasitism is unambiguous,
part of a spectrum of interactions
between body and soul,
breeding mutualism through evolution until
you can't distinguish parasite from host.

Grief is a parasite
eating at the table of your loss,
belching on your disappointment,
ruminating in your memories,
and gradually, leisurely
consuming who you are.

A Dog's Heart

All of God's creatures have a purpose,
whether it's to feed, inform, entertain or enlighten us.
They're all here to give their gifts to the world,
to accomplish their destiny.
From the tiny white lab mouse to the
majestic African elephant, they must
all be given our gratitude and respect.

There is a reason why dog spelt backwards is god.
They were put on this earth to be a human's companion,
to teach us about loyalty, simple pleasures,
perseverance, and to love the unlovable.
A dog's heart is more significant than its mind
and exceedingly far more
brilliant.

My dogs have meant more to me than most friends
I have ever had, for they didn't
judge, belittle, demean, or disappoint me, ever.
They offered me their charm, devotion, comfort and
unconditional love
in a world filled with humans,
incapable of the same.

And that is why I will never go to Asia
or any country whose people have been known
to eat dogs, for they are
not meant to feed our bodies;
they are here to nourish our souls, stave off loneliness,
and to love us
with their enormous hearts.

My Lestat

The Bard of Bonaventure
Lord Byron in bloody black killer boots
Artist, filmmaker, poet, storyteller
Expert in the paranormal, doctors of roots

Flirtatious, friendly, gothic gent
Cologne-doused, confident, sexy as hell
Bi-sexual dandy, kinky, bent
My Lestat, dressed up in jet black

I was drawn, like a moth to a flame
By his passion for knowledge and will to be weird
Adored him for being direct with me, for
No false promises, nothing to be feared

Ball-throbbing blues funk at The Bayou
Snippets of conversational foreplay
Tequila toasts, handholding, deep-throated kisses
I would have followed you, mister, to any old grave

But the sensual Savannahian took me to
Emperors Gentleman's Club
Was I interested in a threesome?
Did I have any ones?

He left me at the bar to buy sessions with pole dancers and
A shooter for a waitress with my forty bucks
I sipped a Moscow Mule and talked to gorgeous Avalon
Wondering what would come next and what the fuck?

Never one to suffer from a lack of imagination
If I wasn't so hetero, I'd have chosen her for his bed
And I went home with this vampire on his invitation
But his familiar cat, Blinxie, had a thing for me instead

After sex, I had a long time to think as he slept
The cock and ball ring raising questions in my brain
Nursed my hangover with Tylenol and aqua from the tap
And wondered, is this how it feels to pay to get laid?

He said all the right things to get me in bed
After five and a half years without intercourse, I bled
My soft hands scratched his back and tickled his bum
If we weren't so drunk and tired, it could've been more fun

No regrets, repercussions but the traffic cop outside his gate
Who pegged me for the Jezebel I looked like at eight
Damn me for forgetting my silver bracelet there
As the spicy scent of my Lestat wafted away in the air

My Pagan Heart

My pagan heart belongs to no world religion.
I cannot put blind faith into the hearts and minds of men.
Reverence for nature leads my spirit to a Higher Power;
it shimmers silver in sunlight, shining through a forest glen.

The red fox and the raven,
the wind in the willows,
the heady scent of lilacs in the spring;
scorching summer sunsets over the Big Rideau,
stars scattered in the inky sky almost sing.

The petrichor, bronze, red and yellow leaves,
the Zen of olive-green moss on my toes,
the festive smell of burning wood;
midnight call of the lonesome loon, and
rabbit tracks formed on freshly fallen snow.

A stroll through autumn-kissed woods,
a swim in a calm, clear loch,
the taste of ripe raspberries on the tongue;
a full moon on a still night and the call of the wild,
the softness of birchbark to the touch.

My pagan heart responds to this evidence of God.
In nature, music is always perfect and the sermon serene.
Here there is no exclusivity, no propaganda, no dogma,
which is why you'll never find me in your
factitious church scene.

Twin Flame

I see my twin flame's image in the dark side of
a gold and gilded mirror, as he holds it to my face
so I see my covert beauty and foremost strengths,
along with my ugliest prejudices.

I see myself in his shadow, curious, compelled to seek
the verity of his existence, to know my perception is echt.
Aware that my romanticized projection may be
unwelcome, I am wary of this infatuation.

I dwell in the light on the other side of the mirror
but fascination for his knowledge, philosophy and
strange, unusual life choices
keep me lingering, just at arm's length.

Intensely drawn to this man, I hardly know,
my intuition tells me we are not soul mates,
but I can't help but wonder what he's here to teach me,
and I sense an existential earthquake is imminent.

I am in awe of his courage to live an
authentic alternative lifestyle, indulging in
every deviant whim of which he can conceive, but I'm
repelled by his politics and self-absorption.

Yang to my yin, he's reflected parts of me I've never known.
Yet I could swear I've met him before
in the pages of a horror novel—an inkling that a fictional
character manifested makes me distracted and uneasy.

What transformation is he the catalyst for in my life?
I sense an alchemical reaction and am unsure about how
much I want to change, but he will show me
what I most desire, as well as what I most fear.

I am neither brave nor foolish enough to follow him further
than that garden gate of exquisite, ornamental iron
because I can see the bloodstains that linger there,
and I'm afraid that blood is mine.

Bombshell

I never want to forget that epiphanous Friday night
when Irene and I talked on the phone for four hours and
discussed Savannah's spiritual hold on me,
my attraction to my Lestat and his role in me
awakening to the reality of the Illuminati.
It has left me feeling like there is a rip in the fabric
of my space-time continuum.
I was so freaked out but at the same time,
realized there are no coincidences and that
everything I've been through in my life up to that moment
was meant to be.

I laid in bed that night, heart pounding in my chest,
stomach sick with H. Pylori, and
I prayed, asking God to forgive me for the poor job
I was doing of it because my mind jumped
all over the place.
I finally understood why my parents had to be Christians
who faithfully prayed for me to keep me from harm
on my quest for the truth.
I am the family member meant to ask the tough questions,
the one with the most evident intuition,
and the one who must learn everything the hard way
so I don't forget the lessons.

All the people I have loved who have passed over
to the Other Side, guide me and ensure
that when it's my time, I get there to join them.
I needed a catalyst to help me find my way to God
after wandering aimlessly through the valley of the
shadow of death for four long years after
my sister died when I wasn't even sure I wanted to live.

God put him in front of me in the form of someone he knew
I'd pay attention to because it was the only way
he could arouse my awareness and make me *really* listen.
I am sure now that I want to live,
I'm good enough just the way I am,
and I truly deserve to be loved.

I know who my angels are, in Heaven and on Earth,
and my gratitude to them shall have no end.
I have had sleep issues all my life,
but I can't go back to sleep now because
I have much lost time to make up for,
much more to learn, many new experiences to savour, and
much love to give before I am laid to rest.
And I don't want to miss a thing.

Red Flags

Rain-soaked, cloudy Sunday in Savannah,
eyes seared with fatigue
and a Patron hangover,
after a sensational party last night
with my brother from another mother,
Philip and his clan.

On Saturday night, I sat by a pool
watching guys play Cornhole, surrounded
by festive, oyster-shucking Capricorn celebrants,
feeling so happy to be there,
partying outside in January with joyful people
and loving my newly adopted Savannah fam.

But today, back at the dead roach Air BnB,
my heart is in my throat,
bile sits on my tongue, and
my stomach roils as
I fight back the tears and ask myself,
why am I here?

Why am I going to be alone,
again,
on my fifty-fifth birthday,
when all I wanted was
companionship and
to matter enough to someone so they'd be there?

Why am I so disappointed that my intuition
was spot on about my Lestat?
I saw all the red flags but hoped with every bit
of my heart, I was wrong,
that he cared about me as a person, treated me like a
friend,
not a one-night stand he never wanted to see again.

Why am I surprised he would drain me dry,
leaving my corpse to rot in the rain without concern
for a proper burial or respect for the dead?
He's a vampire, and that's what vampires do.
Their hearts don't beat.
How could I expect any other outcome?

Because I did. Because I deserve better,
and I thought it was time for a
whole lot of better to come my way.
Maybe it is, and I must wait longer, put away my
foolish attraction to bad boys and man-children,
and give the good guy a chance.

I will keep doing my best
to lead with love,
stand in my power, and
leave my heart open to the possibility
that even though a hard rain is gonna fall,
I may be pleasantly surprised, yet.

Ghosted

I turned fifty-five yesterday.

One hundred and twelve people posted birthday wishes
on Facebook.

But he didn't.

I spent almost three months talking to him on Messenger
and tried to help him promote his business

while treating him with care and respect.

Although I noticed he never asked about me,
I wanted to believe that someday, he would.

He'd flirted with me, screwed me, and led me to believe

he liked me, but when I returned to Savannah,
he behaved as if I didn't matter at all.

I wanted to matter and, most importantly, have his
friendship, but instead,

he ghosted me.

I should've known that a man who spends more time
with the dead than the living

is incapable of earthly emotions.

Still, it fucking hurts, and I feel like a fool, but
I will get over it as I know his behaviour isn't about me,

and someday, someone he cares for will ghost him too.

Predator

You probably think the world owes you something

Because you were adopted
Because you have a small penis
Because you've seen and done things others have not
Because you're constantly pushing the envelope
Because you overcompensate for what you lack

You probably think you're special

Because you're handsome and guileless
Because you're an artist with pen, paint and words
Because you're a Rosicrucian
Because you're awfully smarter than everyone else

Smarter than the women you charm with your smile,
Dyed-blonde locks, a black Italian suit, and your
Endless storytelling

So much smarter than Democripps, Libtards and all
Who disagree with you politically
So much smarter than those not awake to the Illuminati
So smart and desirable that you don't know what a
Complete, caustic bastard you are
So smart that you treat people any way you please
Because you're so goddamn special
And fuck anyone who's not in on the joke

Maybe you know, but you don't care because it's
All a game to you, and you have nothing to lose
Predator with your vampiric visage and
Over-sized reptilian brain
I see you now for who you really are
A man hiding behind his self-made mythology

A self-absorbed man-child who doesn't care about
Treating others with kindness
A selfish soul who'll keep on taking everything
Because you think the world owes you something
You're a ruthless predator
And karma will be your bitch

Vacation

Went to Savannah for the third time within a year,
for a hard-earned, well-deserved January winter break.

Fell in love with its mystery and Southern Gothic charm,
but what it had in store for me was a ten-day heartache.

Spent some precious time with dearly treasured friends;
considered it a place where a snowbird might land.

Envisioned raunchy, sex-filled nights with vampire Lestat;
we'd talked a lot on Facebook after our one-night stand.

I knew he wouldn't be my life's grand love affair;
thought we'd go out on the town to hear live music again.

I'd wear sexy black lingerie he suggested I invest in;
make him smile with my gifts and share whatever
destined.

Instead, I spent $2,800 to spend half my vacation alone,
at a roach-infested Air BnB, watching *Game of Thrones*.

Focused on Jon Snow as my ulcerated stomach churned;
read Bukowski and cried as my cracked heart yearned.

I walked for hours and hours through museums by myself,
trying to believe that art would save my mental health.

Wish I didn't care; he doesn't give a shit about me,
but that's not how I'm wired and why I cannot see.

So here I must sit and be still with the hurt,
until I can get home and go back to work.

Savannah is now sullied, Bonaventure has been burned;
it'll be a helluva long time, if ever, before I next return.

The Glorious Sun

Ahh, the glorious sun!
From the land of lucid dreaming
I wake,
stretch,
throw off the covers and
greet my dog
who lies beneath me beside the bed.

Drawing the curtains,
I welcome a new day,
always more cherished when the sun is glorious
shining through the cloudy thoughts of
mistakes I've made.
The wrong men I've given my heart to,
how stuck I feel in this life—lost more than found,
and how much I miss my sister.

Waking thoughts that are as reliable
as the chubby squirrels
who continue to forage for food
on the pathway behind the
Bowling Greens,
those all-weather rodents who
just go on with their lives
and never let the weather
get them down.

When the sun shines in winter, it casts its rays of hope,
offering strength for perseverance, motivation,
to endure another dark night of the soul.
So, I'll be here to bear witness
to the perfect beauty of the lavender crocus
as she peeks through the cold, hard ground
with her saffron eye and turns her face
towards that glorious sun,
a symbol of courage
as we both face a new day.

Boredom Is a Dangerous Thing

Boredom is a dangerous thing.

It paralyzes your energy,
hog-ties your brain and
smothers your dreams,
reducing you to a mound of despair
trailing the echo of your screams.

Sometimes, I'm so bored with my lonely life,
when no one's here except my doodle,
and she can't give me what I need,
so when I spend day after day alone,
I numb the ache with multiple puffs of weed.

I could do something outrageous at any second
Because I'm so bored by the same demons beckoned;
I'll follow the trail of a conspiracy theory
down the never-ending rabbit hole,
or ponder what I'd get for the selling of my soul.

Sometimes I'm so bored I could cry or smash things,
a ludicrous mad woman wailing like a banshee,
or a pitiful, wounded animal,
howling in pain and anguish,
praying for a bullet or a mallet to the skull.

Boredom is a dangerous thing.

It's pervasive and leads to dire consequences
eats your gratitude, spits out your dreams
and impales your faith upon a spike
until there's nothing left but the sensation
of a house of cards falling in your guts.

I'm bored with the weather,
bored with routine,
bored by politics and of faking self-esteem,
bored with the landscape, bored with food,
bored by social media and bored of the view.

Weariness, ennui, apathy, malaise,
I could die of boredom on these frustrating days.

Yellow Balloon

Saturday afternoon,
sitting on the edge
of our community garden
on a park bench
in the sunshine,
so warm,
so welcome,
after what felt like the longest winter ever,
watching a Syrian refugee boy
play with a yellow balloon
on the far end of the garden—
a simple joy
in a complicated world.

My almost thirteen-year-old doodle
lies contented at my feet,
as grateful as I am
to be sitting outside in the sun,
as I listen to the stunning voice
of Amanda Martinez singing
"Mañana" on my iPhone.

I wonder if Scully is pondering
the miracle of freedom and

security from war
as much as
that young boy could be,
even as his yellow balloon
escapes on the breeze
and flies away to balloon freedom
for which there is no tomorrow,
only today—
only this moment
of absolute perfection.

Lily of the Valley

She may be pretty and
sweetly scented,
the stylish pirate wench who won't
cut her hair,
looks good in photos and
presents well on paper,
but she is not what she appears
to the naked eye.

She hides behind her self-righteous
Catholic shield,
trying to convince herself that her
"Good deeds"
will be enough to get her into Heaven,
while those of us who recognize her
for what she is
are sure she's bound for Hell
because her soul is ugly,
and her heart is
two sizes too small.

She speaks before she thinks,
her words, full of vitriol,
yet you don't seem to notice that or
her lack of empathy, compassion and

love for your children,
but I guess you can overlook that
in favour of her bank account,
which is ironic, considering
she's morally and spiritually
bankrupt.

Narcissism,
like the lily of the valley,
is toxic to those who ingest its
poison
and you devoured it,
knowing full well you'd ignored the
skull and crossbones,
but your foolish decision
didn't harm just you,
it injured your children too
and for that, someday, you will be
very sorry.

Chasing the Dragon

Spring sunshine, green grass, cool breezes,
daffodils and tulips in full bloom,
lift the weight of winter depression
perpetuated by loneliness and
Seasonal Affective Disorder,
as Mother Nature smiles like
the Mona Lisa
and winks.

The fact of my life now is
that there are very few places
close by
where I can sit by the water or
enjoy nature's gifts
because I live in a high-rise overlooking
one of the busiest traffic intersections
in the city.

I can't even enjoy my balcony
because of the noise and exhaust fumes,
and in this siren zone,
I feel as if I'm living in The Bronx
in the 1970s.
The ridiculousness
of this predicament
is beyond laughable.

But it is what it is
for now.
I can't afford to move again
anytime soon,
so, I live like my pet rats,
in a cage,
always trying to figure out how
to escape.

I've spent my life chasing the dragon of happiness
and I get to stroke it occasionally
but then it slips away,
faster than the speed of light,
and I don't know why I bother
trying to catch up with it
because ultimately, it will
breathe fire upon me anyway.

September Sunflower

The majesty of the September sunflower
lies in its ability to always reach for the sun.

Tall, optimistic, and full of goodness,
its rays shine in splendour towards Heaven and,

despite the elements, it remains faithful to its calling,
seeking spiritual knowledge, light and truth,

its yellowness depicting vitality, intelligence, and mirth;
those are things that we humans pray for daily.

The Greek myth of Clytie and Apollo
awarded the sunflower its adoration and loyalty,

Van Gogh recognized its significance long before
the rest of us mere mortals,

as did my sunflower sister
who understands its magnificence,

because she's not bitter or cynical and always
leads with her heart.

Loyal, nourishing, and warm,
she seeks out positivity and

just like the blooming sunflower,
always turns to face the sun.

Immeasurable

PAIN

chronic,

acute,

immeasurable

by anyone

but you.

Right knee,

left hip,

lower back,

right shoulder,

and then

there's the

grief—

never-ending,

torturous,

spirit-changing

grief.

Torn meniscus,

degenerative disc disease,

neuropathic pain,

carpal tunnel syndrome,

piriformis syndrome,

herpes outbreaks,

one after the other.

When

will the

fucking

PAIN

end?

That bottle of

Zopiclone

looks more

alluring

every day.

Federal Election

It's October 2019, and while it's usually this
Halloween lover's favourite month
This year I've endured all the horror I can stand
The crisp, smoke-scented air of fall doesn't comfort me
The changing colour of leaves presents no beauty
The season holds no promise of a new beginning
As it once did—only the beginning of the end

A federal election will be held in twelve days
And no matter who I vote for
The result won't benefit my life in any way
I will still be a prisoner of unfair tax debt
A failing health care system, poisoned food
Skyrocketing rent and the cost of living
That prohibits me from enjoying the life I dreamed of

The world is full of corrupt, greedy corporate leaders
Who don't give a flying fuck about the average person
They only want to ensure their power and dominance
As they systematically destroy the middle class
As ruthlessly as they ravage the earth
They've ruined my entertainment, annihilated my heroes
And stolen my joy

Their plan for a New World Order doesn't include
An intelligent strategy for climate change or poverty
Refugeeism or health care for everyone
Because they won't acknowledge that these issues will
Eventually affect them and the poor
Who they would see perish without care
They're above all that because they are the Chosen

Absolute power always corrupts absolutely
That guy Orwell had it all figured out
And because the world's most powerful
Are the spawn of Satan
They are destined to demolish everything that was once
Positive and pleasurable about life on Planet Earth
And this transition is devastating

The Matrix

Everett,
in the movie, *Paterson* says,
after pulling a fake gun on everyone in the bar,
“Without love, what reason is there for anything?”
I know, Everett... nothing,
not a fucking thing that matters anyway.
Without love, every day is the same damn pandemic day.
Wake up, walk the dog,
make coffee,
drink coffee, read a book,
do housework,
work at the computer, walk the dog, eat lunch,
work at the computer some more.
Make dinner, eat it,
walk the dog,
maybe phone a friend,
watch Netflix,
go to bed.
Get up the next day and
do it all over again—
in pain.
For what?
How many useless facts can I hold in my head?
I forget more than I learn,
every day,
so little of it matters.

Without love,
there's no reason for anything.
Without love,
every day's a pandemic day.
Without love,
we don't really exist.
It's all just the matrix.

I Make Lists on My Phone

I make lists on my phone—
notes from Brené Brown's books,
my shame inventory,
favourite TV shows,
who I consider myself to be,
my top fifty books,
what I want for my life,
ideas for poems about COVID-19,
affirmations,
qualities had by the guy of my dreams,
men I can remember sleeping with,
what's important to me,
recipes, quotes,
psychic medium readings,
parks to visit for nature walks,
friends who awoke,
Christmas card recipients,
how to control emotions before a full moon,
people in my life I value and miss,
ideas for courses,
films by Jim Jarmusch, and
my bucket list.
I make lists on my phone—
that's all you need to know.

Three Hundred, Sixty-Five Days Wrong

Snowpiercer, one thousand, thirty-four cars long;
COVID pandemic, three hundred, sixty-five days wrong.

Today it is St. Patrick's Day, and I want to slit my wrists;
however, Wilford Industries has nothing to do with this.

Mandatory mask misery, fear-based news,
third-wave virus variants, what nocuous vaccine to choose.

Lockdowns after lockdowns after lockdowns,
destroying self-made careers and businesses in every town.

Lost friendships, lost livelihood, and lost ambition;
so tired of anxiety, terrene boredom, and depression.

Cannot see the light, nor can I see the sun; I've aged
no less than ten years during this last dreadful one.

Cannot feel warmth, can't envision the future,
of all those numb, broken hearts so badly needing sutures.

Winter of the spirit, dark night of the soul;
if I could find the damn abyss, I would jump into its hole.

Netflix-induced nightmares, body pain for months,
insanity-inciting headlines shatter my every want.

Cannot make my dog feel calm when I do not feel safe,
from the dictators and oligarchs controlling our fate.

Where will we be by the year 2030?
Will Bill Gates and the eugenicists win by playing dirty?

FUCK YOU, billionaires, Big Pharma, Big Tech too,
I just want this stupid shit to end and to see the end of you!

Invisible

When you're a single, middle-aged, overweight woman,
you're invisible.
You could steal a fifty-five-inch TV from Best Buy, and no one would even notice.
No one looks your way, asks you about your day,
hugs you just because or wonders what once was.
No one sees you, your heart, mind, value, or accomplishments,
except for maybe your closest friends, if you are most fortunate.

People do not ask you about your job, your hopes and dreams,
or what is on your bucket list—
not even your family.
Maybe they're too busy or too tired to care;
maybe they have no room in their lives
for lovers or new friends.
Or maybe they're just self-absorbed or simply pitiful fools,
or maybe there is just too much infernal pain in the world.

When you're a single, middle-aged, overweight woman,
you're a ghost in society,
even if you're talented, successful, and kind,
a good listener, or a romantic
who cares for her fellow man and this great big blue planet.

You're still a spectre—a faceless mass in a crowd—
a persona non grata,
someone whose ship has sailed,
you might as well wear a shroud.

The best years of your life are behind you,
and no one cares about your stories,
so why bother to write them down?
No one cares about what you have to say.
No one cares about what you might do,
or who you might save or if you'll be wooed.
You're simply invisible, and if you are a
single, middle-aged, overweight woman—
you know that this is true.

The Consequences of Your Decisions

Once upon a time, I was a bold, adventurous,
outgoing woman who took risks.
I lived in various cities,
learned more jobs than I can count,
travelled whenever I could,
and had
a boatload of friends.

Always able to make new pals,
I was the hostess with the mostest,
a natural networker,
bringing people together,
spending everything I had to
enjoy their company,
living for fun and joy whenever possible.

Everything is different now.

It has been a year since I've seen some of my
closest companions,
and over two years for more.
A few longtime chums don't feel safe
seeing me now,
as I'm unvaccinated—a pandemic pariah—
because I don't feel safe being a human guinea pig
for an experimental gene therapy "vaccine."

I don't trust our government, Big Pharma or Big Tech,
or the 1 percent Elite who have been holding us hostage
for a virus that has killed less than 0.058%
of the global population over the last eighteen months,
and who have caused far more collateral damage
than that, with their political divisiveness,
lockdowns, mandated masks and ordered vaccines.

My sister died from ovarian cancer
because she couldn't tolerate the chemo drugs.
My mother experiences adverse effects from many
medications,
and I was recently diagnosed
with an autoimmune disease
for which there is no data
to prove the safety of the vaccines for me.

But choosing to care for
my immune system naturally
now makes me
a fool, and worse,
someone who doesn't care
about others in society
or for the greater good.

Or does it?

"We can still talk on the phone, and
we'll forever be in each other's hearts," she said.

"Everyone makes their own choice, and they have to
live with the consequences of their decision," said Mare.

The consequences of my decision...

It will keep me from seeing my friends,
from travelling,
from going to the gym or museums,
movies or concerts,
restaurants, stadiums,
and anywhere
that large crowds gather.

Now, I am a quiet, introverted,
anxious woman who is
going nowhere.
I have a few faithful friends
and the only risk I'm taking
is in not getting
the jab.

Foolish Stories about Love

In this life, we are told foolish stories about love:
that love conquers all,
it's better to have loved and lost than never to love at all,
that the more love you give away, the more you have,
if you set it free and it comes back, it's yours.
But not everyone experiences that.

There was once a young woman with so much to give,
that she gave and gave and gave it away,
not always expecting love in return, but she was hopeful.
Mostly, she hoped her love would be enough
because she knew she was far from perfect,
and it was cumbersome for her to carry alone.

Perhaps she was not discerning enough
or amply careful with her gifts of love,
yet her heart was true, and her flame burned from her truth.
So, she took her chances and gave her heart to many
who she assumed would appreciate it, benefit from it,
heal with it, even treasure it.

However, her love was not always cherished,
nor valued or reciprocated, and
her heart was not filled with more love.
Neither was the weight of it lifted.
Instead, she was left tired, weak, worn out, burnt, parched,
callused, jaded, distrustful, and cynical.

Eventually, after carelessly giving her love
to so many humans who did not want or appreciate it,
to too many humans who abused it and left it to rot,
she realized that her well of love was empty, and
her love dried up and, like a crisp, rusty autumn leaf,
disintegrated and blew away in the wind.

Sometimes there's a limit to one's love and hope.
Sometimes love is not enough, and sometimes
no matter how long we wait
or how diligent we are about cultivating love—it just
doesn't grow—
it is not replenished; it does not come back to us,
and it does not create more love.
Love simply dies,
and we never know if it will reincarnate.

Christmas Nirvana

The second Coronavirus Christmas Day is here.
Freezing rain outside is just another reminder
that travel is not recommended.
Eloise and I sit in my living room this morning,
and I drink dark roast coffee and
read beautiful Buddhist poetry by Emily Maguire,
as my Goldendoodle girl watches Nature TV for Dogs
on YouTube,
reminding us that the resonance of nature
is the most perfect sound in the world.
She watches the Canada Geese goslings and their parents,
the majestic swans with their cygnets,
the Mallards and their ducklings
—with interest—all of them eating, quacking, swimming,
and honking while birds sing in the background—
a symphony of summer magnificence.
I catch myself watching them too,
especially the swans, which are surely the
most spectacular species of bird on the planet.
Did you know they can walk on water,
just like Jesus, miraculous,
on the Sea of Galilee?

As they glide effortlessly across the lake,
I am reminded that freedom and simplicity still exist,
that nature is God's greatest gift,
and that no plandemic can ever take its solace away.
The skies may be grey outdoors today,
but inside,
it is Christmas Nirvana.

Become the Observer

This seeker is an empath;
a truth seeker,
always striving for more
knowledge and understanding
of a world
she's been at war with—
in her mind—more lately
than ever before;
searching for something that will
give her faith in God,
hope for the future,
relief from grief.
At fifty-seven years of age,
she finally realizes
that the truth has always
been within. All she
needed to do
was listen closely
and start over again.
Become the observer,
step outside of external dramas,
go inside her heart,
become neutral and
let her higher self show her
the right moment
to stop fighting, and
to help others.

The secret is
there is no absolute truth;
everything in the Universe
is permitted as part
of its evolution. When we
become the observer,
we enter the eye of the storm,
connect with our hearts,
and therein, we find
love and harmony.
There is well-being in
our shadow selves,
so there is no need to ignore
as the body operates in tandem
with the subconscious mind.
There is peace in silence,
and when the noise of humanity
invades the quiet,
nature and sound healing
help seal the cracks.
Don't take life too seriously;
enjoy the journey,
dream big,
love yourself,
follow your interests, and
LET GO of anything else
that doesn't resonate.
You are all that and
a bag of chips—
you are the observer,
the great I AM.

A Stone in My Boot

My soul recognized itself in every man I ever loved.
I chose men who were handsome, kind, fun,
creative, damaged,
addicts running from their demons—
running from themselves and their past—
who were utterly incapable of loving themselves or me.
It took until I was fifty-eight years old to figure out that
because I couldn't love myself, I tried to love men
who were just like me, equally tainted,
to try to save them. However, I couldn't save them
because I couldn't save myself.
I couldn't love myself.
I was already damaged from being sexually molested
by my father's half-brother when I was thirteen.
By then, my father couldn't even communicate with me,
let alone protect me and keep me safe.
So, it didn't matter that by the time I was seventeen,
I gave my virginity away to someone who didn't deserve it,
and who I didn't love, or that
I slept with over one hundred men after him.
It didn't matter because I didn't matter.
They hurt me, lied to me, cheated on me,
and took advantage of me and my kind heart.
But that was nothing that I wasn't already doing to myself.
For so long, I've thought that men constantly hurt me,
and always will, so I keep them at bay.
But it was me who hurt myself repeatedly.

I am still an addict; I am still damaged,
I am still chasing my demons,
And I still can't find a way to love myself genuinely,
No matter how many spiritual, philosophical or
Psychological self-help books I read.
Every day, I walk with a stone in my boot.
Every day, I put one foot in front of the other,
And try not to limp.

Wasteland

Another quiet snowy night, and I can't sleep.
I hate Canadian winter, but I like quiet nights like this,
even though I sleep less and less
as the months of the pandemic slip by—
twenty-two of them now.
We're in lockdown again in Ontario—for the whole
month of January—
maybe longer, and this nightmare...
JUST. WON'T. END.

I've been so full of anxiety and anger
about watching humanity be robbed of
its' health freedom,
that my dog appears not to love me.
I've had her for twenty-five months since she
was ten weeks old.
She's not often comfortable with me
and seeks affection rarely, making me lonelier
than I have ever felt being separated from humans.
I am not the person I was when my other dogs
loved me.
That breaks my bleeding heart.
I've tried so hard with this dog to give her
everything I can,
and she's never alone, but it's never enough.
I walk her to the dog park at minus twenty Celcius,
wearing two pairs of pants, a sweater, a puffer coat, a hat,
mitts, and boots, and it's not enough.

The guilt I feel for being an emotional basket case,
and causing my dog anxiety is slaying me.
She may well be a mirror for me,
but I can't bear to look at what she reflects.

I try to calm my shattered nerves and broken heart
by reading Brené Brown after midnight,
trying to find something positive in this shitty situation.
In *Atlas of the Heart*, she writes,
"Connection is in our neurobiology.
This is why our experiences of disconnection are so painful
and why chronic disconnection leads to social isolation,
loneliness, and feelings of powerlessness."
Our leaders are slowly and systematically killing us
with their management of a super virus,
and I feel so goddamn powerless to change anything.

My feelings, your feelings, our feelings
are meaningless to them as they continue to push
their fear-based mind control to make us
submissive, acquiescent,
accepting of their decisions without questioning them.
Thank God more people question them every day,
because they've got it all wrong.
So little of what's unfolded has made any rational sense.
They've led us into social isolation,
loneliness, and feelings of powerlessness.
They've led us into a frozen wasteland
of an existence that becomes increasingly less tolerable
with every sleepless night.

I don't want to feel this way anymore.
I just want my dog to love me.
I want to feel joy and freedom to do what I want to.
How can so many people still sleep at night
in this fucked-up world?
How can you not resist or revolt,
but simply allow the 1 percent Elite to take our lives
away from us indefinitely?
I can't be alone with my insomnia anymore.

I need something tangible to live for.
I need to touch a friend's shoulder in a pub
as I get out of my chair and walk, maskless,
to the bar to buy pints for us while a rock band plays,
and sings its heart out for a live audience.
I need to know I can get on a plane and go to
the Caribbean,
if I could afford to, if the pandemic hadn't wiped out my
business and left me exhausted,
and at serious risk of losing my will to live.
I want out of this frozen wasteland immediately!

Let it be known that my death will be on you,
Ford and Trudeau, Fauci and Gates, you soulless
psychopaths, not that you'd give a shit.
Oh no, you don't have concerns about anything
but your egos, your money, and your power.
May your black souls rot in Hell for eternity.
At least I'm consoled by the fact that when I'm dead,
either from or with COVID, or by my own hand,
my traumatized dog won't miss me.

Leghold Trap

Like a fox caught in a leghold trap,
I'm ready to chew my foot off.
Anything to free me from this prison.
After thirteen years of working from home in social media,
four months of going absolutely nowhere,
two years in a global pandemic under totalitarian rule,
and two months of Canadian winter,
I am as anxious and depressed as I've ever been.
Some days, I feel like I'm losing my mind, as all I do
is cry and ruminate on my half-chewed-out psyche
and ever-expanding waistline.
Some days, I manage to smile or laugh and remind myself
to be thankful that I'm not physically or sexually abused.

Cabin fever has this fat fox going insane from the guilt
of not being grateful enough for the pretty cage she lives in,
and ironically, is constantly worried she'll lose.
Isolation and lack of culture and community
is seriously sapping my will to survive.
What good does it do to fight mass formation psychosis
if I have to give up everything?
If I make it to spring without being hospitalized
or locked in a morgue fridge, it will be a miracle.
I need this shitstorm to end right fucking NOW.
I'd vote for the Conservatives if it got us out of this.
I want my freedom back.

Touch

> "The thought of that would come to me sometimes, and I would think I kent what Jesus must feel like there—so wanting, and no one to touch Him."
>
> ~ *Jamie Fraser,*
> *A Breath of Snow and Ashes* by Diana Gabaldon

It has been three and a half years since anyone
has touched me beyond a friendly hug.
Before then, five and a half years,
and seven months before then, when my
friend of twenty-six years who I thought I was in love with,
broke my heart. All were one-night stands,
even he who I had held so dear, and
loved from afar for so long.
Before him, it had been over five and a half years
since any man had held me in his arms,
stroked my cheek, caressed my skin,
or kissed my lips with ardent want.
Such starvation for human touch shatters the soul.
The deprivation leaves us less than—
less than whole, less than cherished, less than loved,
less than seen, less than wanted—
less than who we could have been.
There is no food, drink, drug, or possession
that can make the yearning for human touch disappear.
I know because I've tried everything. And yet,

I do not want to be treated as less than ever again.
I do not want to be used and discarded,
like so much disappointing, flavourless food
left to rot in a rubbish bin. I don't want to be good enough
for a one-time shag and then left forever by the next man
who goes on to search for someone better,
because I wasn't the one. To live in this paradox,
day after day, month after month,
year after year is shaving years off my life
with a dull razor.
Every day, I find myself with just a little less will
to live than the day before. When even my dog cannot
give me the affection I crave; I know I am not
who I once was and will never be who I could have been
if I'd had someone to touch me more.

You're in the Mediocre Zone

You're in the Mediocre Zone if you tend to focus on the problems.

You're in the Miracle Zone when you're invited to play a more fulfilling game.

The miracles that you are seeking are seeking you.

The Miracle Zone is where you live in grace.

You deserve the good fortune that you most desire.

Shift from ego-based to soul-based intentions.

List ten things you want to create.

Identify which ones are ego-based and which are soul-based.

Shift the language of your intention into your soul.

Harness the phenomenal power of the thoughts of those around you.

Our thoughts are more potent than our words.

Maybe too many people in your life have thoughts that do not support your happiness.

Surround yourself with people who think positively.

Write down a list of people in your life, and break free from the worst offenders.

Know and own your inherent worthiness.

When you don't feel worthy of receiving, you energetically push miracles away.

Do not deflect compliments.

Accept gifts with gratitude.

When things are great, celebrate your success.

Self-esteem is not self-love—you must love yourself.

Increase your awareness of how you push good away.

Expand your ability to receive right now.

Open, breathe to receive, and feel gratitude in your heart.

Don't let fear make you avoid taking the steps you know you must take.

Your commitment to yourself must come from your heart.

You Are Unsinkable

You are unsinkable.

Let go of the past.

Reprogram your conscious mind.

Your thoughts are causing your suffering.

You can only think of one thing at a time.

Think of what you want and not want you don't.

Write your goals out.

Gratitude will turn things around.

Raise your vibration for the day.

Believe. Behave. Become.

Shift your thoughts, and you will shift your life.

What are you thinking right now?

Turn your thoughts into positive stories.

Reprogram your subconscious mind.

Elevate your vibrational frequency.

Like energy attracts like energy.

Get yourself to a state of love, peace, joy, and gratitude.

You are pain-free.

You are open to financial abundance.

You are open to receiving the love of your life.

Surrender to what is.

Let go of the past.

You don't manifest what you want.

You manifest what you believe.

We do not die; we simply transition.

Sinkhole

I'm up and down like a flipping yo-yo.
I can't go back.
There's no hot tub time machine.
No access to a parallel world where I am fit, loved
and happy.
I spend every moment in this Now,
trying to put one foot in front of the other,
taking one day at a time.
I can't plan for my future,
my mood turns on a dime.
I can't count on anyone but myself.
No restorative sleep, no respite from extremes.
I can't get my feelings validated,
I can't take proper care of myself.
I can't pay my taxes.
I can't listen to my intuition
because I don't like what it says.
Life is never going to get any better.
The best part has passed me by.
I let it happen.
I put others' needs before my own,
but they won't do the same for me.
What is it going to take to make a change?
How can I find the silver lining when I don't know
if I believe in miracles?

The more I learn, the less I know.
I can see the red flags, all the baggage I tow.
I can't decide if a fundamental part of being human
and alive is to choose between being afraid
or being angry.
I can't be sure of anything.
I'm stuck in this sinkhole.
I can't go back.
There's nowhere to go.

I Am Not a Victim

I am not a victim.

I am not overly sensitive.

I am not too emotional.

I will not tell the same story of what's wrong repeatedly.

I will not seek allies to validate what's wrong in my life or the world.

I will not gossip.

I will not play the blame and judgment game, express indignation, or lash out.

No one has to change for me to be happy, consequential, or peaceful.

I will not behave with superiority or think I am better than anyone else.

I will not use spirituality as a crutch.

I will not spiral into overwhelm and anxiety.

I will trust my intuition.

I will stop thinking I need to protect myself.

I will honour my feelings and tune into the facts in a healthy detached way.

I will understand what triggered me.

I will shift the energy using a healing tool like sound vibration or classical music.

I will let any negative feelings go.

I will decide my next action by connecting to my soul.

Death Is Drinking My Tequila

Night after night,
I watch TV alone.
My dog often lays under the bistro dining set
or maybe in her bed in my room,
but never close to me
because she doesn't want me nearby
unless I have chicken or cheese in my hand,
or her leash.

I've wasted at least three years of my life watching TV,
and it means nothing—it's just
BioFreeze for an often lonely existence.
I shift uncomfortably in my recliner for hours,
picking up my phone, wasting time
on stupid apps that don't matter,
or making lists of things I want to remember,
or reading books that will hopefully be good enough
to keep me from
writing a less-than-glowing review for an author
that may be a Twitter acquaintance,
who will block me if I dare share my honest opinion.

I don't know why I watch so many dark shows
Like *Rome*, *Ozark*, *Succession* or
Game of Thrones,

because they're all a testament
to the bane of Homo sapiens,
to the depths of their depravity,
to their barbaric nature, and
to the bitter disappointment
that is the human race.

No matter how hot the men are
or how beautiful the women,
the characters are wretched,
miserable, greedy murderers who treat
life like a chess game,
but with more disdain.
So much darkness.
Death is drinking my tequila
while I stare at the balcony lights
thinking, what the hell am I doing?
Turn this shit off and go to bed.

Get Out of Your Head

Get out of your head now.
Get into your body, start living your life again,
stop overthinking everything,
and open the damn champagne!

You spend too much time trying to avoid
how uncomfortable you feel in your body,
feeling sorry for yourself and desolate,
unloved and unsupported.

You are good enough no matter your weight,
and you always were,
so get out of your head, *stop thinking*,
get into your body, and live!

You have been kicking and raging
against maturing for a decade
since you decided to be true to yourself
and lost most of the friends you'd made.

You cannot turn back the clock,
you don't know how to time travel,
or transport your spirit to a parallel universe,
no matter how much you read about it.

For the love of the Higher Power
you say that you believe in,
Just bloody well surrender,
and get out of your head now.

Do all you want for pleasure,
work and be with people too.
No more pressure, no I'm not enough,
is allowed for you, you fool.

Self-loathing is not welcome here,
release all that does not serve you.
Be the best version of who you are
and fulfill your sacred purpose.

Don't Forget to Tell the Aliens

The best thing about being human is our sense of taste.
Just try explaining to an alien
how blue cheese and sliced cherry tomatoes
with mayonnaise on black pumpernickel almost melt in
your mouth, each bite like a symphony
of stinky-sweet, earthy, rich delectability.

Or try describing to that Grey,
the sensual flavour of smoked salmon and cream cheese
with chive on an all-dressed bagel
—a savoury taste sensation for the ages—
that could surely lure the Zeta Reticulans
from their flying saucers.

Tell them they wouldn't want to miss out
on the creamy, moderately crunchy, slightly tart
but smooth dichotomy
of egg salad with Hellman's and Dijon mustard,
chopped celery, dill pickles,
or green onions on a crusty bun.

And don't forget to tell those aliens
how sensational a spicy siesta of chipotle chicken salad
with avocado, chopped tomatoes, green olives,
jalapenos, and spring greens
in a flour tortilla
will flamenco dance on the tongue.

Or about Brandt's Liverwurst with Herbs
on a sourdough baguette, and
tuna salad mixed with diced pickles or onions,
seasoned with salt and pepper,
and a dash or two of Frank's Buffalo Hot Sauce
with old cheddar melted on toasted ancient grain bread.

For the sake of the Universe,
don't forget to tell the aliens about
the succulent juiciness of a messy sloppy joe
made with taco-seasoned ground beef,
roasted bell peppers, mushrooms,
onions and cilantro on a cheese bun!

Because those big-headed, black-eyed,
skinny-armed, earless,
telepathic communicating,
abducting little Grey freaks
are never going to leave
when you conclude with...

Ooh! Last but not least,
the sublime satiety of a classic Black Forest ham
and Swiss cheese with Hellman's and baby spinach
on Rudolph's rye, which, together with a road map,
will save your day and get you
where you're going.

There is nothing quite like the tiered design
and strategically placed ingredients in these perfect,
tasty, quick-to-make choices for any meal.
The deliciousness of sandwiches and a bag of Dill Pickle
Kettle Chips should explain to those aliens why being
human makes us the happier, superior species.

Fucking James Purefoy

I cannot quite get over
what is shown
on cable television
or streaming channels
these days.
Nothing is sacred.
You can learn how to build a sex room,
how gigolos earn a living,
learn sex education through teenagers' eyes,
and watch adults fucking
while having affairs repeatedly.

I'm not a prude; I never was regarding sex.
I'm not wildly kinky
(you'll never know that much about me),
but was a naughty girl when I was younger,
going through men like a revolving door.
It has been so long; I don't recognize that person anymore.
I only have vacation sex once every five years,
whether I need to or not.
It's the only time I feel like, why not?
I can be anyone I want—I am on vacation.
I will never have to see him again;
he won't owe me anything.
I'll be wasted and blame my actions on tequila.
No one will ever know unless I tell them.

All my lovers are ghosts of the past,
either departed or alive.
They show up in my dreams occasionally,
just to let me know they never forgot me.
They never loved me enough to stay with me,
but they never discounted me.
I guess that is something.

It's so rare that I watch a show or movie,
and an actor makes me think about coitus—
actually makes me horny—
but nine times out of ten,
it is James Purefoy.
He seems like a lovely, thoughtful man
when I listen to him in interviews,
but I don't remember that guy when I see Purefoy
letting Christina Hendricks ride him on a beach
in *Hap and Leonard*,
Marc Antony ploughing Polly Walker's Atia of the Julii
in *Rome*,
or as the disturbingly sexy serial killer, Joe Carroll,
seducing his cult followers
in *The Following*.

What's wrong with me?
Why do I find strong, charismatic bad boys
so ridiculously enticing,
even when I know better?
Even when every other part of me has evolved spiritually,
when it comes to sexual attraction,
I still behave like I am eighteen
and hope the next time will be different—end differently.

Like most viewers of this lurid sex on TV,
I can't quite pull myself away from viewing it,
even as I question why the hell I'm watching.
But one of these days,
I am going to give up goddamned TV
and get a real life.
I will get out in the world and find a real man,
like James Purefoy,
and remember why I liked fucking in the first place.
And I will be sober when I do it.

Swans in the Mist

I moved into a cheap thirty-five-year-old condo building
in the second summer of the pandemic.
The hallways were sad and somewhat dingy
but relatively clean.
Fourteen hundred dollars was all I could afford
for a small two-bedroom.

I had to get away from the insane traffic noise,
and frequent car crashes
where I had been living
on the corner of Bath Road and Sir John A.
I couldn't stand the energy there anymore;
I was losing my mind.

The building I moved to overlooks a
marshland conservation area,
abundant with wildlife, and
I became transfixed by a swan couple who lived there.
Their majestic beauty inspired me;
their presence soothed me with serenity.

I looked for those swans every morning
in the creek of the marsh,
and when I saw them, it was a good omen.
Some mornings, the sun shone on the water,
shimmering diamonds, air lavish with birdsong,
and I hoped Romeo & Juliet would grace me
with their presence.

One grey Halloween morning, when the fog was thick,
the cattails were brown, and all the colours
of the marsh were muted,
I stood on a hill overlooking the water,
waiting for my dog to do her thing, I saw
Romeo & Juliet silently glide down the creek in the mist,
leaving a gently rippling trail in their wake.

The beauty of that moment was so surreal and profound
I think of it to this day—
a cinematic film noir masterpiece—
in which no one is murdered.
Mated Mute swans following each other down the stream,
slowly disappearing from view, off to their elegant life;
it was one of the most perfect moments of mine.

My Father is a Christian

I remember the day Karen called to ask me,
had I heard the unbelievable news?
"Dad asked Jesus to be in his heart."
I thought that Hell must have lost its muse.

A stranger thing I could not have dreamed of,
though Mom waited thirty years for that moment.
For twelve years, he has tried to get me to subscribe
to a religion I cannot relate to or consider cogent.

He tries to make up for the error of his ways,
working for the church, giving assistance to its members,
Eighty years old, out helping others every day,
but no time to talk to me for five minutes, for pleasure.

He will never know how to communicate with me,
but reads his Bible devotedly every day,
believing enough prayer will make up for
all he failed to do for his relations along the way.

I confess I like him better since he was baptized;
he doesn't goad me anymore to be mad at him.
Dad's duties to the church will always come first,
but I forgive him, since my father is a Christian.

Never Take for Granted

Never take for granted
Your right to privacy or that
The news is genuine, or
Perception the same for everyone

Never take for granted
Your right to travel or congregate
Celebrating milestones with friends
Or your claim to a good night's sleep

Never take for granted
That your life will hold amusement
That you can take a course in person
Or apply focus and concentration

Never take for granted
Disinfectant wipes or toilet paper
Or that you'll enjoy live entertainment
While living in the matrix

Never take for granted
That you can trust the government
That there isn't a Great Reset or
That your leaders are legitimate

Never take for granted
You'll have access to healthcare
That your hair will not fall out or
A new vaccine is worth the fanfare

Never take for granted
The food upon your table
That you can afford a place to live
Or see everyone in your bubble

Never take for granted
Passing someone on the sidewalk
The comfort of a loved one's hug or
Freedom to choose any dialogue

A Capricorn's Rap

She's not an intellectual
She's intuitive and visceral
Her morals are not circumspect
She's compassionate and diligent
Her drugs are recreational
She's apathetic, ineffectual
Her vagina isn't satiated
Libido hasn't been sedated
Her men are not emasculated
She cannot be emancipated
She's not a Wiccan Priestess
Her religion is duplicitous
She believes, however, ironically
Her magic's in her veracity
Her ideologies vivisect
Phantasmagoria she can't forget
She's not explicitly political
She's acquiescent and hospitable
Her nihilism is not contagious
She's enigmatic and licentious

Isolation

Lying in bed late at night, I try not to let my thoughts
Get as dark as a black hole in space
Swirling down, down the cosmic funnel
Of infinity, never to land in a sun-drenched meadow
In June 1987, where I awake among the wildflowers
A warm breeze blowing through my hair
And start all over again as a beautiful, confident
Hourglass-shaped, size fourteen blonde girl
With a dream to produce rock music videos

Sometimes being alone with my thoughts
Is like being trapped in a float tank
In the middle of a panic attack
Screaming inside my head for someone to
Lift the lid and let me out
But no one comes, and though
I claw at the roof until my fingernails bleed
I cannot get out of the prison
Of my thoughts and circumstances

CBT teaches us that we can change our thoughts
And as a result, we can change our emotions
So I tell myself I won't think about how I feel
A hungry, caged tiger in forced isolation,
Deprived of freedom, love, movement
And endless possibilities, ready to rip the
Throat out of whoever opens the door

With my fangs and
Just keep running

No, I will think of Bukowski
Sitting at his Olympia, drunk on wine,
Smoking, his face an ugly minefield of acne,
Typing out his daily thoughts about
The mundanity and absurdity of his crazy life,
Droll, sometimes witty, often content with being insane,
While his cat rubs up against his legs, thinking,
"Some people never go crazy.
What truly horrible lives they must lead."

No, I will think about how much worse
My life would have been if I had been born
A woman in the sixteenth century
Treated like chattel, forced by my father
To marry who he chose, even if I didn't know him
Not allowed to learn, read or speak my mind
And how the odds of my dying in childbirth or
From tuberculosis would be at least five to one
And if I rebelled, I could be burnt at the stake

Suddenly, I feel calmer about my pretty cage,
Succumb to the Zopiclone sandman,
Turn off the light and try to get comfortable
Lying on my left side, my arm under my pillow,
Right arm cradling another and let
My clenched jaw loosen as I eventually
Drift off to sleep
Hoping I'll find the sun-drenched meadow in June 1987
And that Dusty will be waiting for me

www.ingramcontent.com/pod-product-compliance
Ingram Content Group UK Ltd.
Pitfield, Milton Keynes, MK11 3LW, UK
UKHW020140250726
13967UKWH00002B/768

9 781738 729623